Migrating Animals

Salmon

B.J. Best

Cavendish Square
New York

Published in 2017 by Cavendish Square Publishing, LLC
243 5th Avenue, Suite 136, New York, NY 10016

Website: cavendishsq.com

This publication represents the opinions and views of the author based on his or her personal experience, knowledge, and research. The information in this book serves as a general guide only. The author and publisher have used their best efforts in preparing this book and disclaim liability rising directly or indirectly from the use and application of this book.

CPSIA Compliance Information: Batch #CW17CSQ

All websites were available and accurate when this book was sent to press.

Library of Congress Cataloging-in-Publication Data

Names: Best, B.J.
Title: Salmon / B.J. Best.
Description: New York : Cavendish Square, 2017. | Series: Migrating animals | Includes index.
Identifiers: ISBN 9781502621023 (pbk.) | ISBN 9781502621047 (library bound) | ISBN 9781502621030 (6 pack) | ISBN 9781502621054 (ebook)
Subjects: LCSH: Salmon--Juvenile literature.
Classification: LCC QL638.S2 B4475 2017 | DDC 597.56--dc23

Editorial Director: David McNamara
Copy Editor: Nathan Heidelberger
Associate Art Director: Amy Greenan
Designer: Alan Sliwinski
Production Coordinator: Karol Szymczuk
Photo Research: J8 Media

The photographs in this book are used by permission and through the courtesy of: Cover Peter Mather/Getty Images Entertainment/ Getty Images; p.5 UnderTheSea/Shutterstock; p. 7 Sergey Gorshkov/Getty Images Entertainment/Getty Images; p. 9 Danita Delimont/ Getty Images Entertainment/Getty Images; p. 11 Portland Press Herald/Getty Images Entertainment/Getty Images; p. 13 Josh Humbert/Getty Images Entertainment/Getty Images; p. 15 Darryl Leniuk/Getty Images Entertainment/Getty Images; p. 17 bikeriderlondon/Shutterstock; p. 19 Momatiuk – Eastcott/Getty Images Entertainment/Getty Images; p. 21 Jeff Foott/Getty Images Entertainment/Getty Images.

Printed in the United States of America

Contents

Salmon are large fish.

They live in cool water.

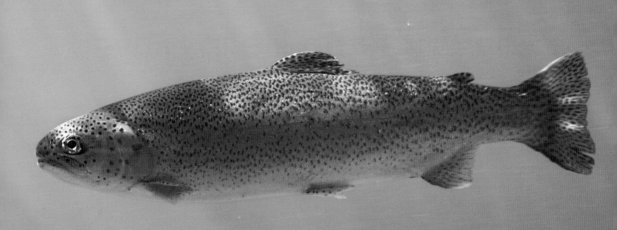

5

Salmon begin life in a river.

They **hatch** from eggs.

Baby salmon are called **fry**.

The river has freshwater.

You could drink it.

9

The baby salmon get older.

They are known as **smolt**.

They begin to live in salt water.

10

11

Adult salmon live in
the ocean.

They live there for about
four years.

Adult salmon go back to where they were born.

They swim to the same river!

15

Salmon are strong.

They jump up the river.

17

Salmon make new eggs
on **gravel**.

The adult salmon are tired.

They die.

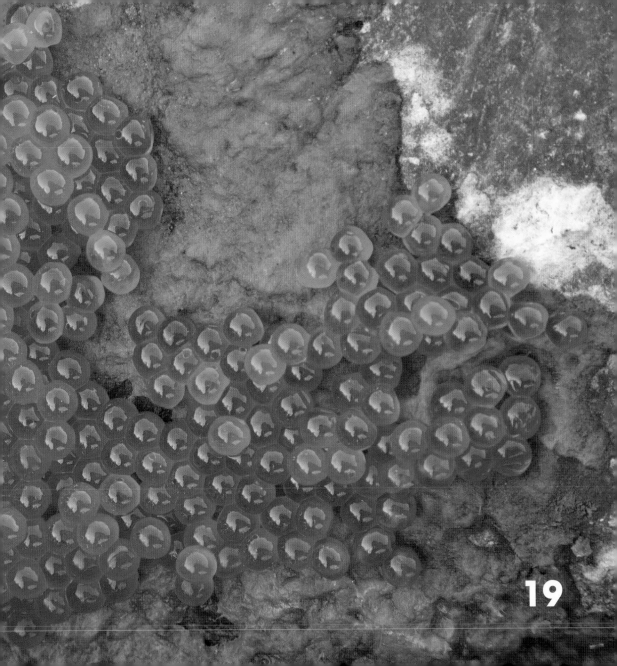

Fry will hatch.

The baby salmon will grow up and leave.

But someday they will come back!

21

New Words

fry (FRY) Baby salmon.

gravel (GRAH-vul) Small rocks.

hatch (HACH) To come out of an egg.

salmon (SAM-un) A large fish.

smolt (SMOHLT) Young salmon.

Index

About the Author

B.J. Best lives in Wisconsin with his wife and son. He has written several other books for children. He has caught fish, but never a salmon.

About BOOKWORMS

Bookworms help independent readers gain reading confidence through high-frequency words, simple sentences, and strong picture/text support. Each book explores a concept that helps children relate what they read to the world they live in.